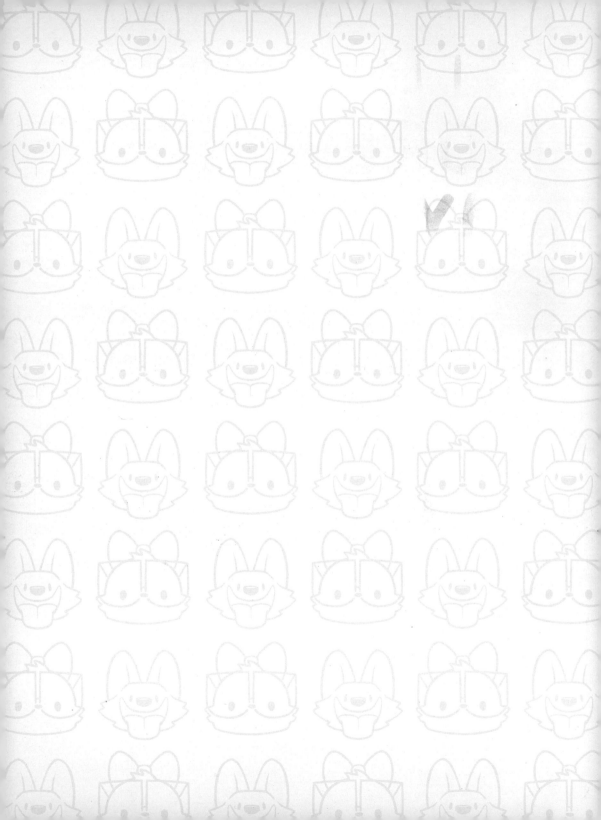

I LOVE YOU MORE THAN MY PHONE

A "SLOTHILDA & PEANUT" COMIC COLLECTION

DANTE FABIERO

Skyhorse Publishing

FOR K.C. & FREDDIE

TABLE OF CONTENTS

INTRODUCTION

I love my phone. It entertains me when I'm bored, wakes me up in the morning, and helps me navigate my way through life ... literally, I'd probably be lost on the streets right now if it weren't for GPS.

Interestingly enough, all of the above could also be said for my dog, Peanut ... well, except for the GPS part.

This love for both my phone and my dog served as the inspiration for my online comic series, "Slothilda & Peanut." Slothilda is a sleepy little sloth who's obsessed with her phone, snacks, and naps. Admittedly, she's a caricature loosely based on my wife and me.

Cartoon Peanut the corgi, on the other hand, is pretty much exactly like Peanut, my real-life corgi—a direct reflection of my stumpy-legged goober.

In this follow-up title to my first book, *Slothilda: Living the Sloth Life*, I dive deeper into Slothilda's world, exploring the hilarious and loving relationship she has with her endearing canine—a compilation of vignettes about friendship, as well as the adorable mishaps of pet-parenting as told through the eyes of Slothilda.

Peanut can be quite the handful at times. He craves attention to no end, loves eating whatever he can find, and wishes fireworks would be banned from this Earth. But, he's also the most blissfully devoted companion and best friend anyone could ever ask for; exactly how he is in real life. So, while he may lack built-in satellite technology, Netflix, and Instagram, I'll never waver when tell I him: "I love you more than my phone." In these comics you'll see that Slothilda feels the same way, and I hope you do, too.

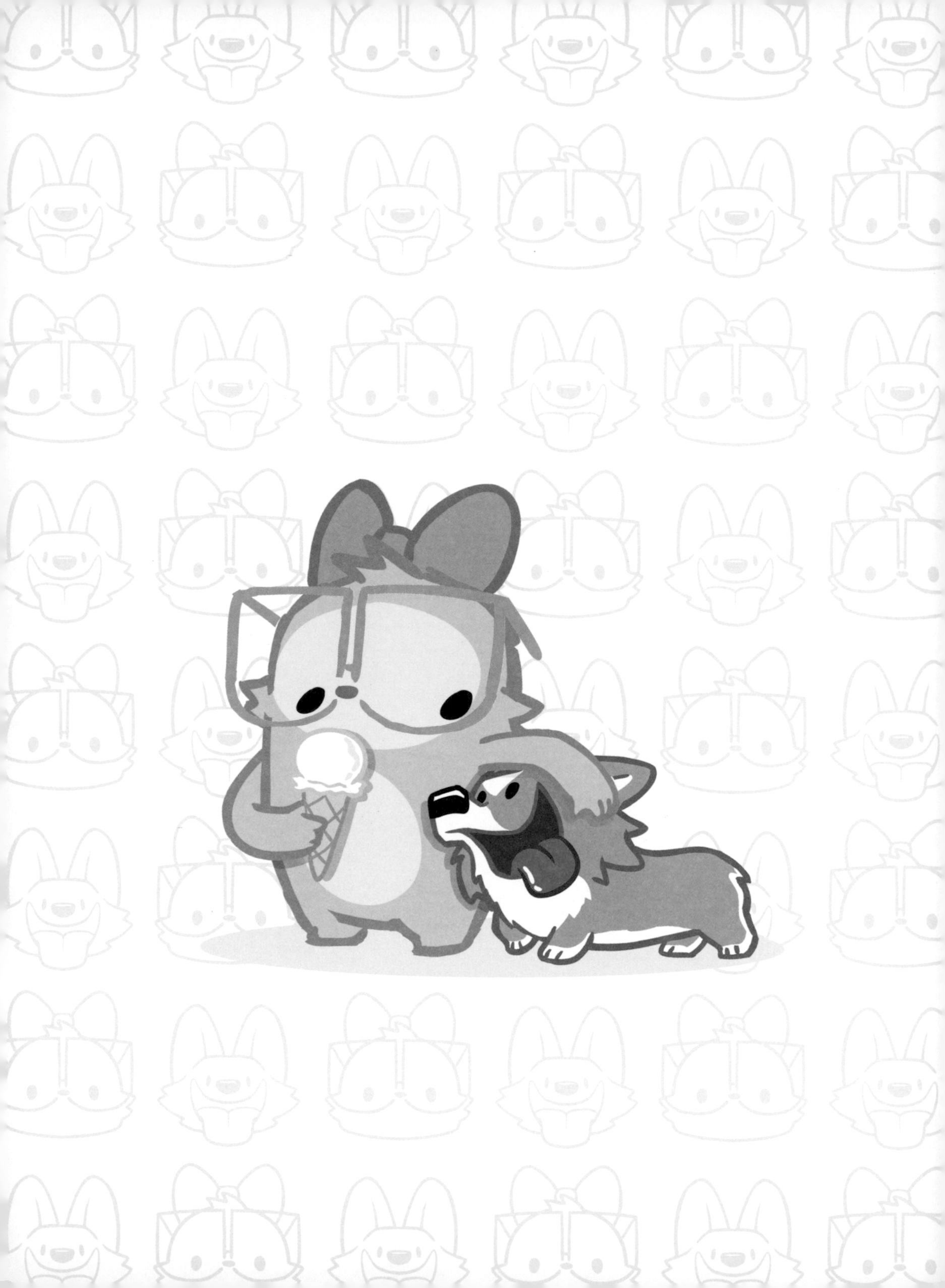

SLOTH'S BEST FRIEND

HOW TO TELL IF YOUR DOG WANTS A BELLY RUB

1. HE FOLLOWS YOU

2. HE BEGS YOU

3. HE GIVES YOU NO CHOICE

PEANUT'S HARMLESS.

COULDN'T EVEN HURT A FL—

TECHNICALLY...THAT WAS A GNAT.

WHATCHA DOIN'?

WHATCHA DOIN'?

WHATCHA DOIN'?

4

AMOUNT OF TIME IT TAKES
TO BATHE PEANUT = 20 MINUTES

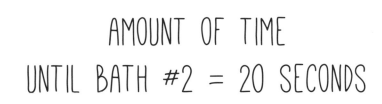

AMOUNT OF TIME
UNTIL BATH #2 = 20 SECONDS

"INTRUDERS," ACCORDING TO PEANUT

GOPHERS

SQUIRRELS

FERAL CATS

CROWS

SWEET MS. BAILEY

SOMETIMES I USE A FOOTREST WHILE I WORK.

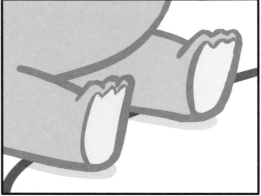

OTHER TIMES...THE FOOTREST USES ME.

YOU THINK PEANUT HAD SOMETHING
TO DO WITH IT?

I HAVE A HUNCH.

PEANUT THE PROTECTOR

MY HOUSE WARDEN

MY BODY GUARD

MY PARK RANGER

MY SECURITY BLANKET

I LOVE PEANUT'S PUPPY DOG EYES

JUST NOT WHILE I'M EATING.

CORGI CAMOUFLAGE

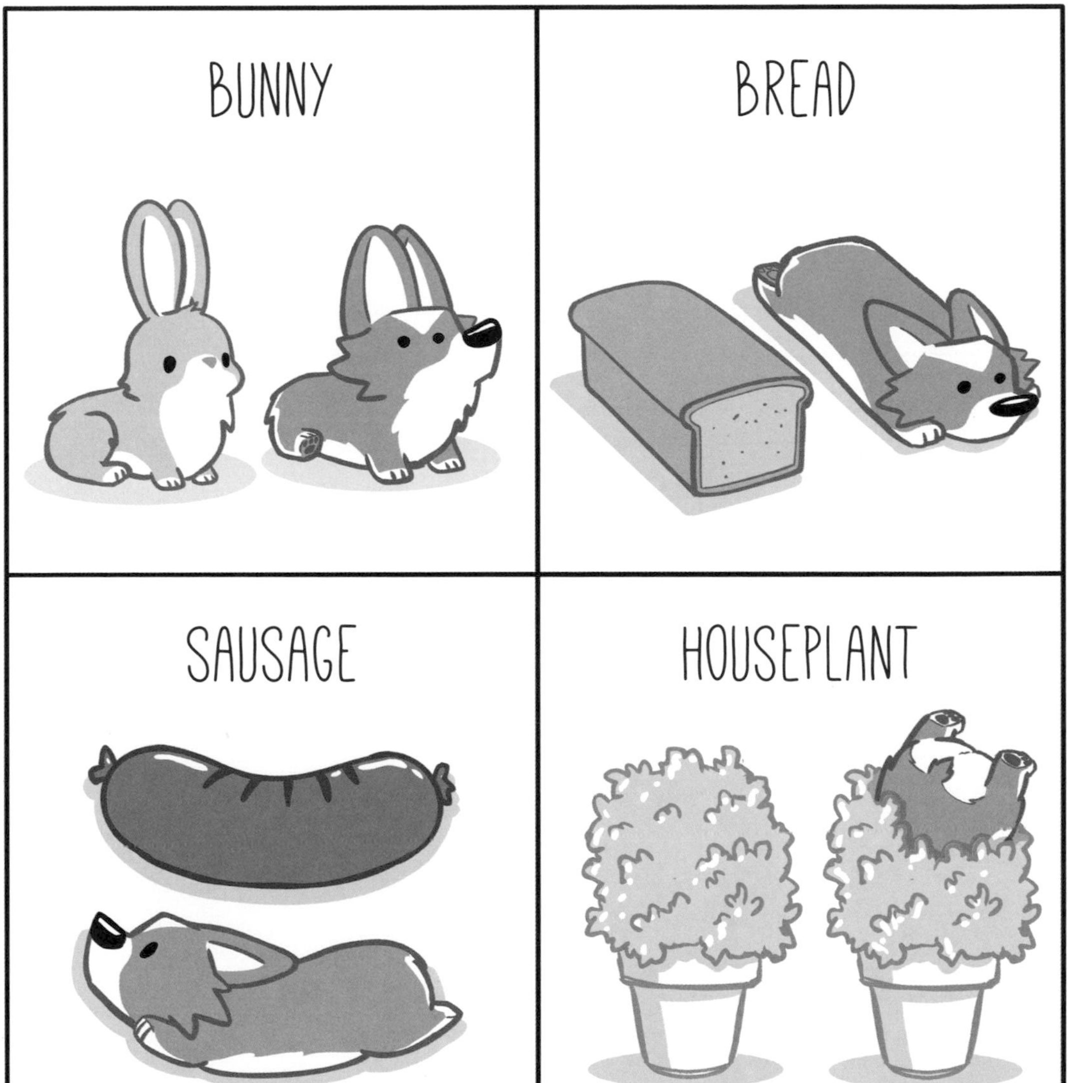

BUNNY
BREAD
SAUSAGE
HOUSEPLANT

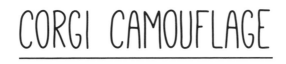

LIFE ISN'T ALL RAINBOWS AND UNICORNS,

BUT WITH THE RIGHT TOOLS...

ANYTHING IS POSSIBLE.

THE MANY ROLES OF A DOG

1. MY BEST FRIEND

2. MY FUR BABY

3. MY GUARD DOG

4. MY TRUSTY MOP

HOW PEANUT BEHAVES DURING THE DAY:

HOW HE BEHAVES AT NIGHT:

I BUILT YOU A NEW DOGHOUSE, PEANUT!

DIDN'T BUILD THAT, BUT OKAY.

PEANUT, I GOTTA GO.

SEE YOU LATER. I'LL MISS YOU.

I CAN TELL YOU'LL MISS ME, TOO.

PEANUT DOESN'T JUDGE A BOOK BY ITS COVER.

HE JUDGES IT BY ITS FLAVOR.

YOU GET ONE DONUT, PEANUT,

SO CHOOSE WISELY, OKAY?

SOMETIMES I TRICK PEANUT...

AND SOMETIMES IT COMES BACK TO BITE ME.

FOURTH OF JULY ESSENTIALS

FIREWORKS

HOTDOGS

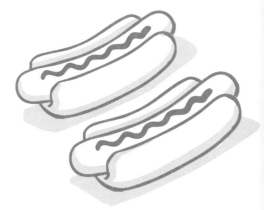

MUSIC

NOISE-CANCELLING HEADPHONES

DOGGY EXPRESSION GUIDE

"I LOVE YOU."

"DON'T LEAVE."

"CAN I HAVE SOME?"

"SANDWICH? WHAT SANDWICH?"

HAVE YOU SEEN MY CREDIT CARD?

PEANUT, YOU'LL NEVER KNOW

WHAT IT'S LIKE TO BE IN MY SHOES.

I MEANT FIGURATIVELY.

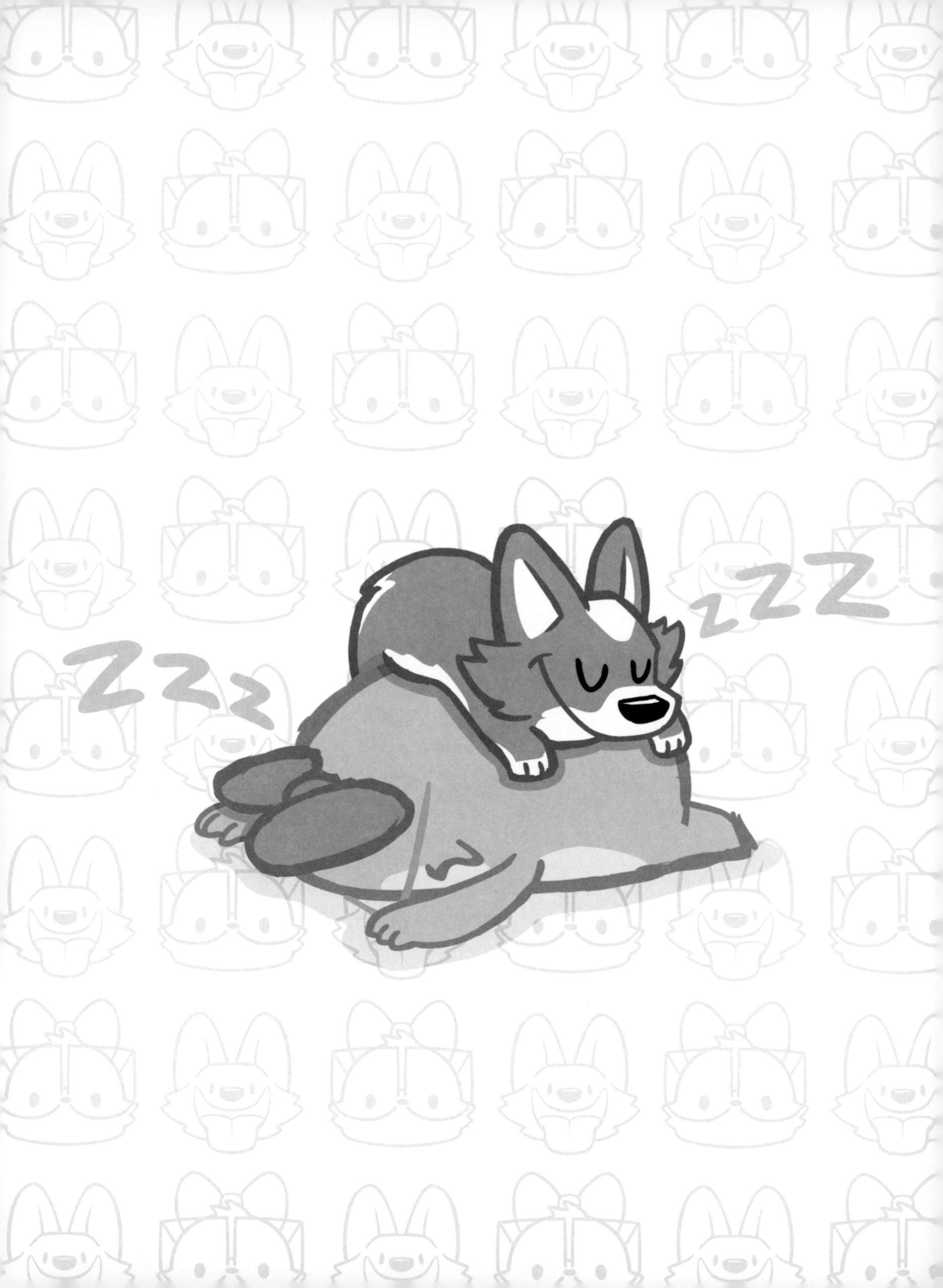
ZZzz
zZZ

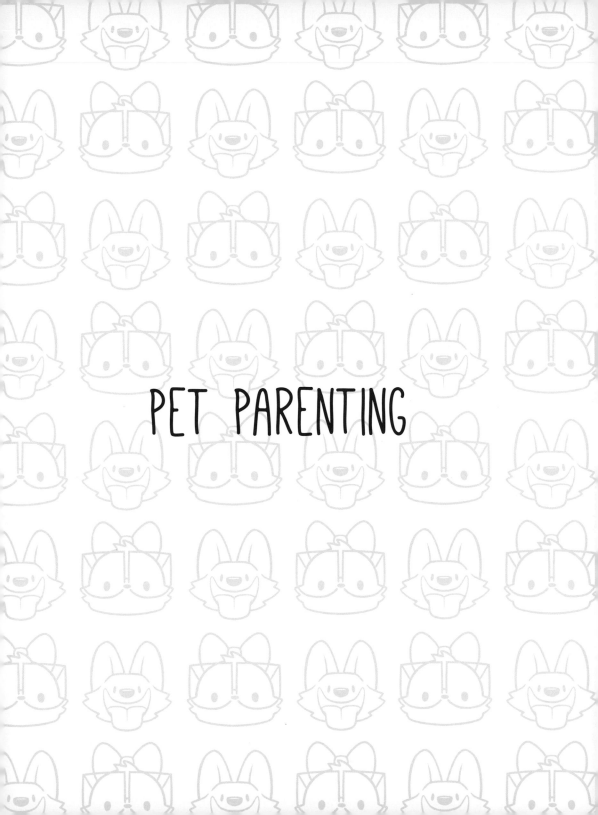

PET PARENTING

PEANUT, ALWAYS PREPARED FOR

PLAY TIME

WALK TIME

MEAL TIME

BATH TIME?

HOW TO EASE YOUR DOG'S SEPARATION ANXIETY

1. TIPTOE PAST THEM

2. LEAVE A TREAT

3. SNEAK OUT QUIETLY

4. CLOSE THE DOOR

5. WORK FROM HOME

TAKE THAT LEAP OF FAITH, PEANUT.

THE FIRST STEP IS ALWAYS THE HARDEST.

THE DO'S AND DON'TS OF DOG CARE:

PEANUT NEVER LETS GO OF THE BIG STICKS.

THANK GOODNESS.

HOW TO CALM AN ENERGETIC DOG

1. GO FOR A LONG WALK.

2. PLAY WITH A FRISBEE.

3. SOCIALIZE WITH OTHER DOGS.

MONEY DOESN'T BUY HAPPINESS

BUT IT DOES FOR PEANUT.

HOW TO TELL IF YOUR DOG HAS A FOOD ALLERGY

1. HE GETS ITCHY

2. HE GETS GAS

3. HIS MOOD CHANGES

4. YOU RACK UP A $400 VET BILL

GEEZ, WATCH YOUR STEP, PEANUT!

PAY ATTENTION, WHY DON'T CHA?

HOW TO KEEP WARM IN THE SNOW

1. BUNDLE UP

2. DRINK HOT COCOA

3. SNUGGLE

4. GET OUT OF THE SNOW

I LOVE YOU MORE THAN MY PHONE, PEANUT...

BUT LEMME PUT THE CASE ON FIRST!

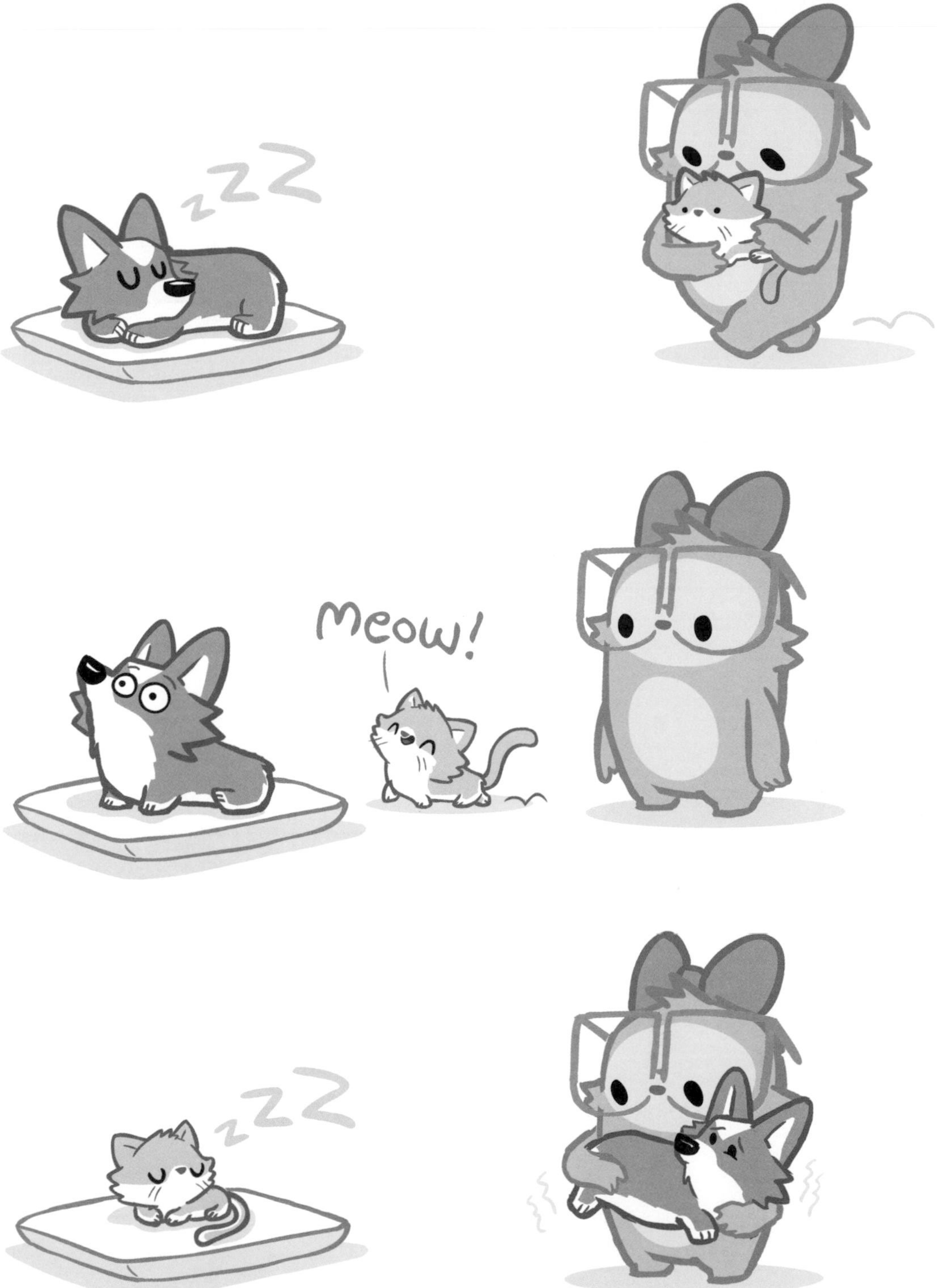
zZZ
Meow!
zZZ

NEVER BITE OFF MORE THAN YOU CAN CHEW...

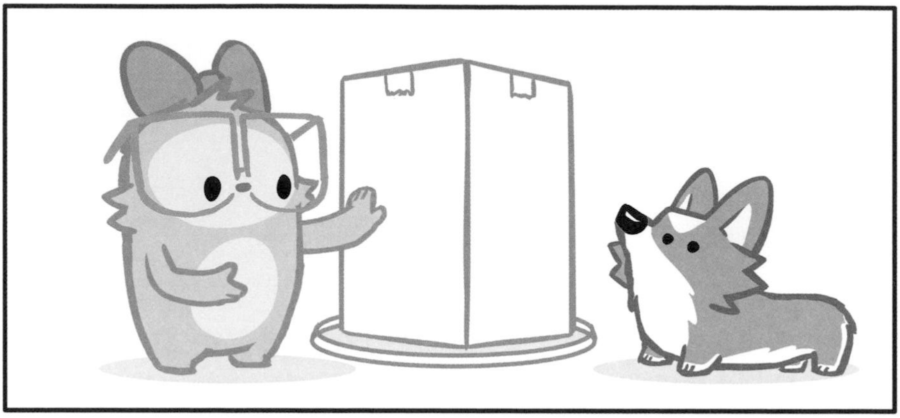

...UNLESS IT'S CAKE!

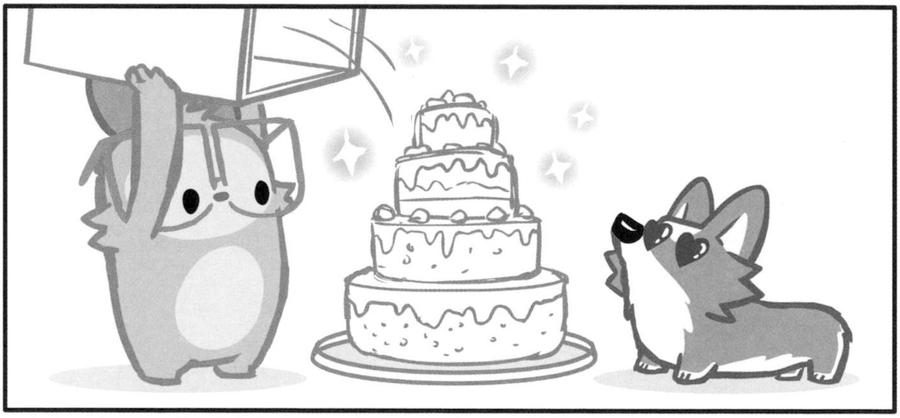

CHEWING IS OPTIONAL.

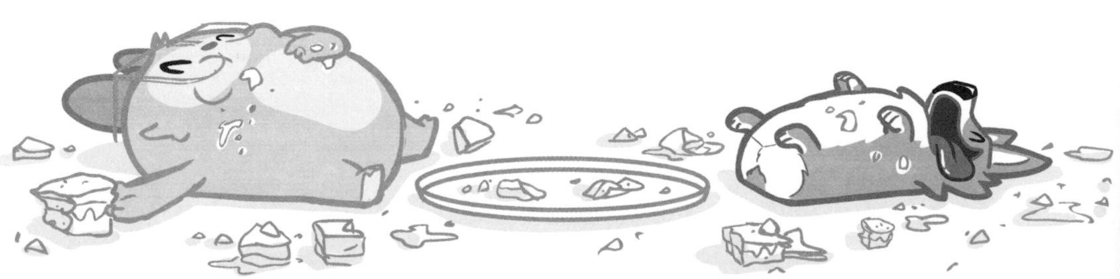

REACH FOR THE STARS, PEANUT...

BUT PLEASE HURRY UP.

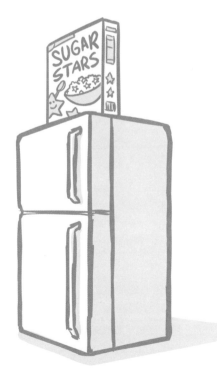

IT'S IMPORTANT WE BE MINDFUL

AND PRESENT.

FUN THINGS TO DO WITH YOUR DOG

GO ON A PICNIC

GO FOR A RUN

GO TO THE BEACH   PLAY IN A SPRINKLER

THEY SAY DOGS CAN READ YOUR EMOTIONS,

BUT I'M NOT SO SURE.

PEANUT, SIT.

PEANUT, SIT!

SERIOUSLY, PLEASE SIT.

PEANUT LOVES GOING ON HIKES,

ESPECIALLY WHEN HE DOESN'T HAVE TO.

A PICTURE IS WORTH A THOUSAND WORDS...

IF YOU CAN ACTUALLY GET ONE.

IT'S OKAY, PEANUT. YOUR FAVORITE RIDE...

...HAS NO HEIGHT REQUIREMENT.

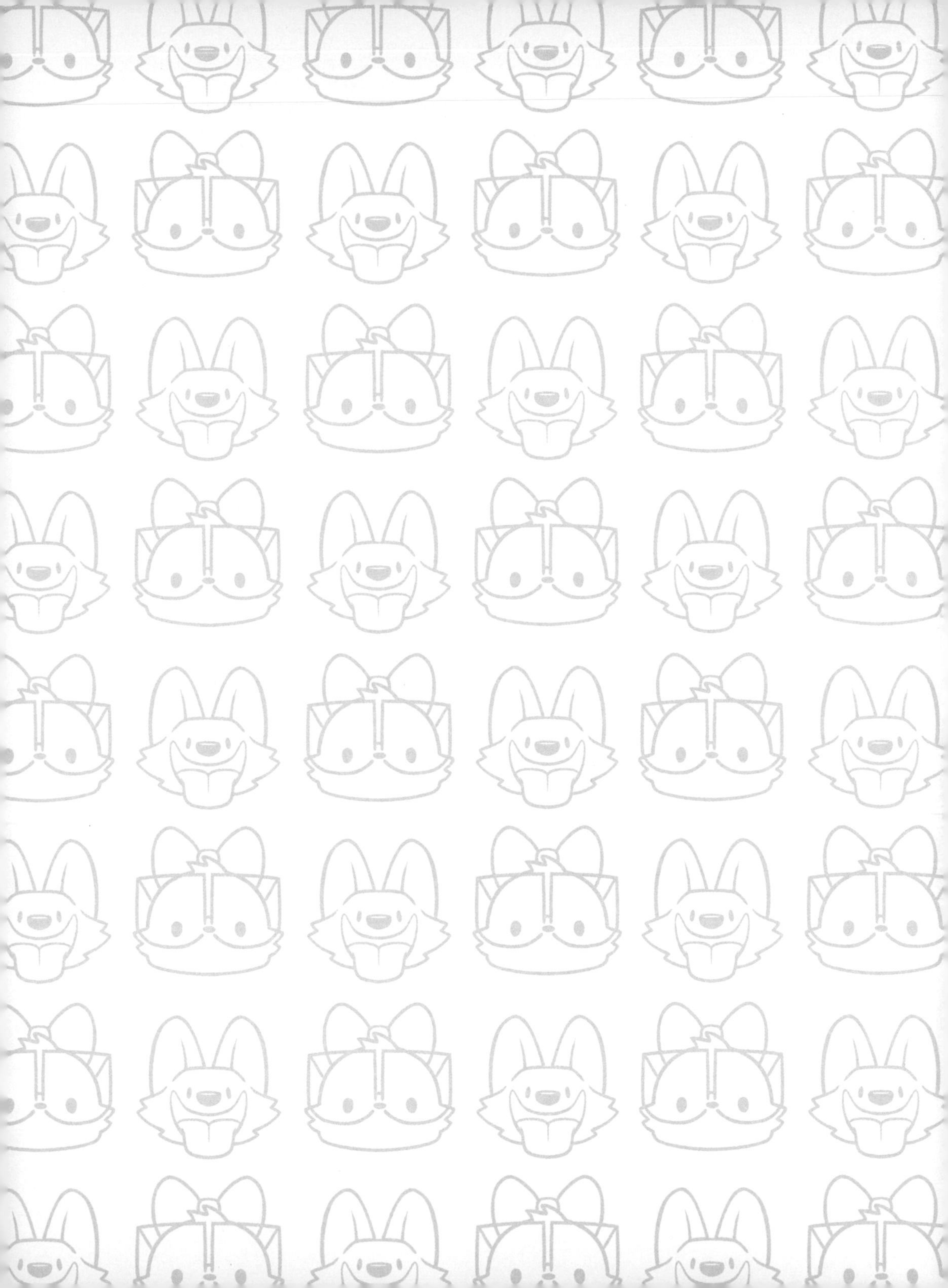

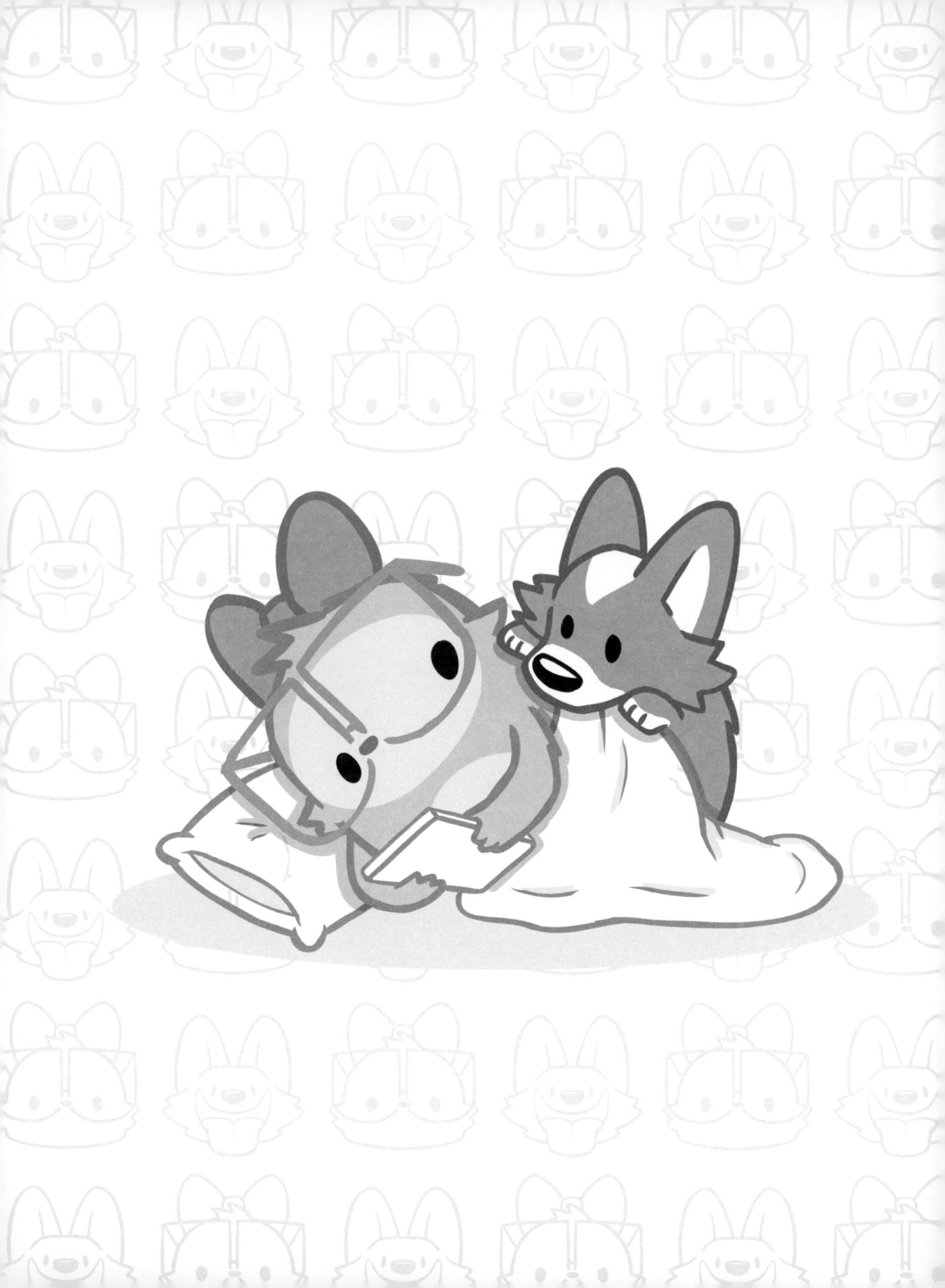

HOME SWEET HOME

COME QUICK,

THERE'S BEEN AN ACCIDENT!

NUMBER TWO, LIVING ROOM CARPET.

I'M DISAPPOINTED IN YOU, PEANUT.

BUT ALSO, VERY
IMPRESSED.

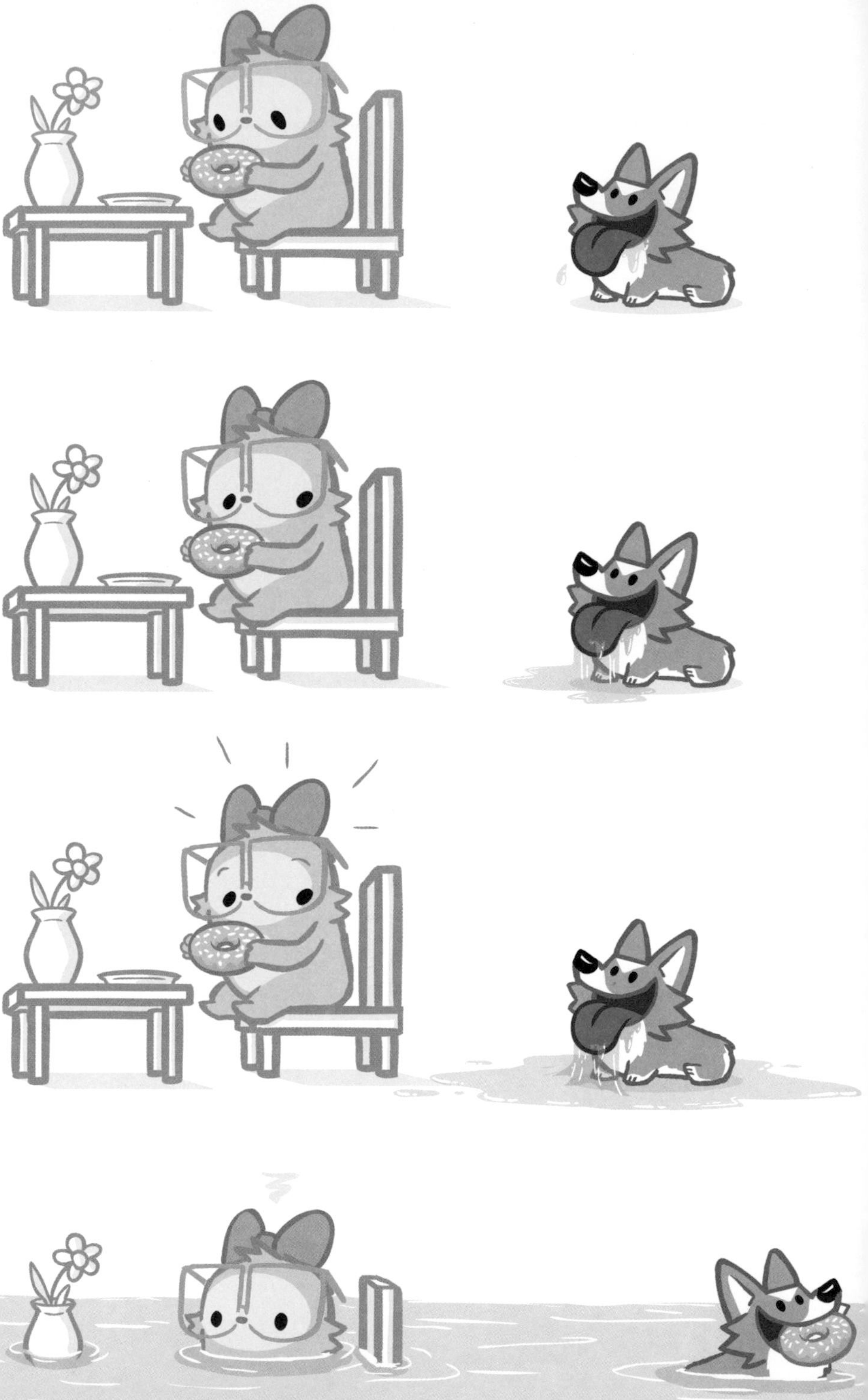

LET SLEEPING DOGS LIE.

THE COUCH IS MORE COMFORTABLE ANYWAY.

GOOD JOB, PEANUT!

YOU'RE MAKING PROGRESS...

BUT CAN WE AT LEAST GET PAST THE DOOR?

IT SAYS HERE THESE TREATS
HELP IMPROVE DOG BREATH...

...THOUGH RESULTS MAY VARY.

PEANUT LOVES TO WATCH ME...

1. TAKE A BITE

2. TAKE A NAP

3. TAKE A TUMBLE

NO, PEANUT! ANYWHERE BUT THE RUG!

NEVER MIND.

ROBOTS.

CAN'T BEAT 'EM?

JOIN 'EM.

ENJOY YOUR NEW BED, PEANUT!

IT COST ME A FORTUNE.

MY TOILET, A.K.A.

A DRINKING BOWL

A HEADREST

A STORAGE UNIT

A LOUD NOISE SECURITY SHELTER

PEANUT SEES AN IMPENETRABLE WALL.

I SEE A COST-EFFECTIVE BARRIER.

CHECK OUT MY NEW...

DUST BUSTER!

OR NOT.

SOMETIMES PEANUT JUST SITS
AND STARES FOR HOURS.

I WONDER WHAT HE'S THINKING ABOUT.

WHAT HAPPENED?

CAT GOT YOUR TONGUE?

ACTUALLY...CAT GOT **MY** TONGUE.

SILLY PEANUT.

ALWAYS DOING SILLY THINGS

WITH THAT SILLY PENCIL.

THEY SAY THE TOUGHEST CLIMBS LEAD
TO THE NICEST VIEWS.

I DISAGREE.

FUN THINGS TO DO WITH A BLANKET

MAKE A TENT

MAKE A WALL

MAKE A CURTAIN

MAKE A DARK ROOM

PEANUT REALLY WANTS TO GO OUTSIDE.

HE'S BEEN DROPPING HINTS ALL WEEK.

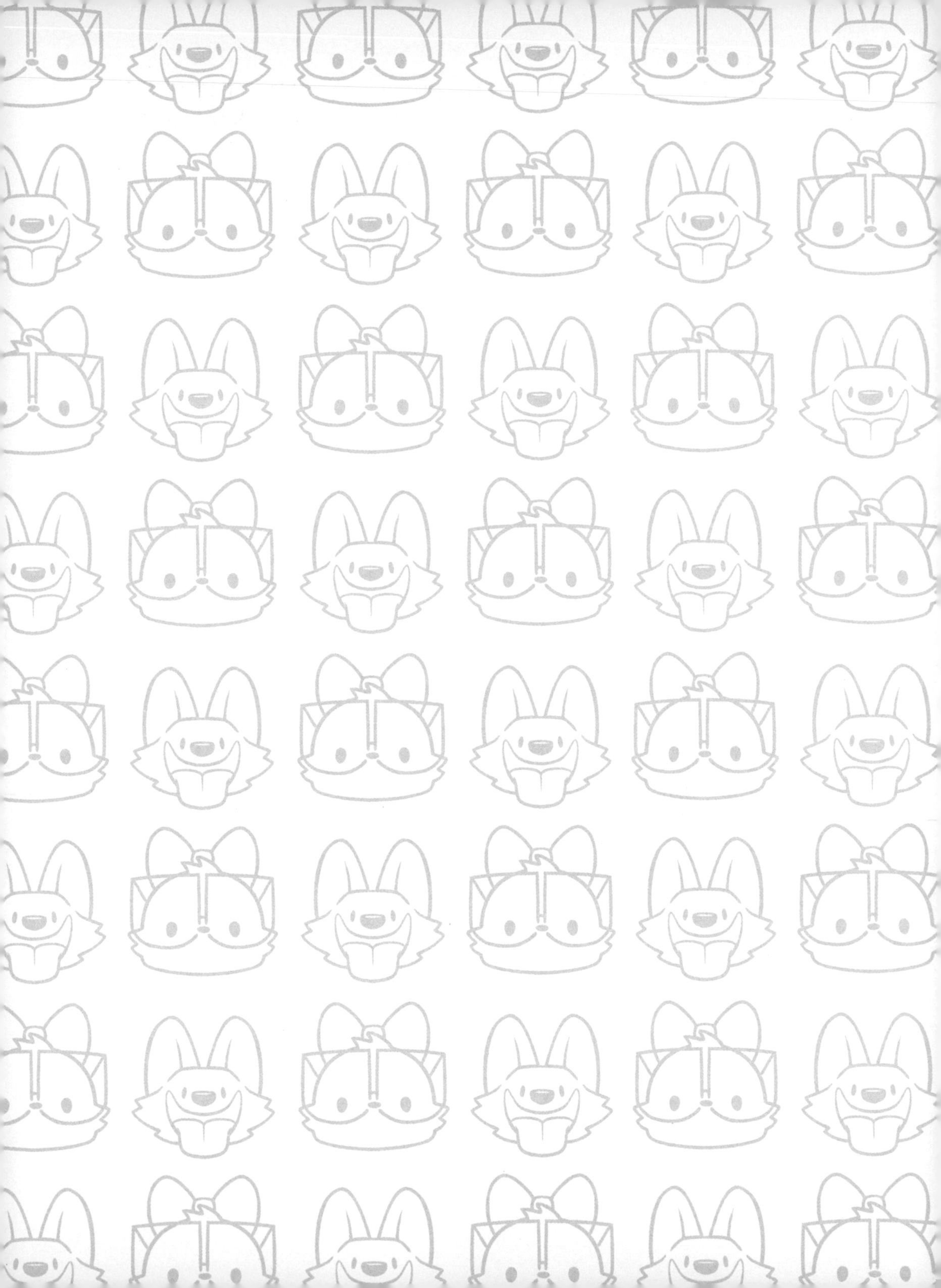

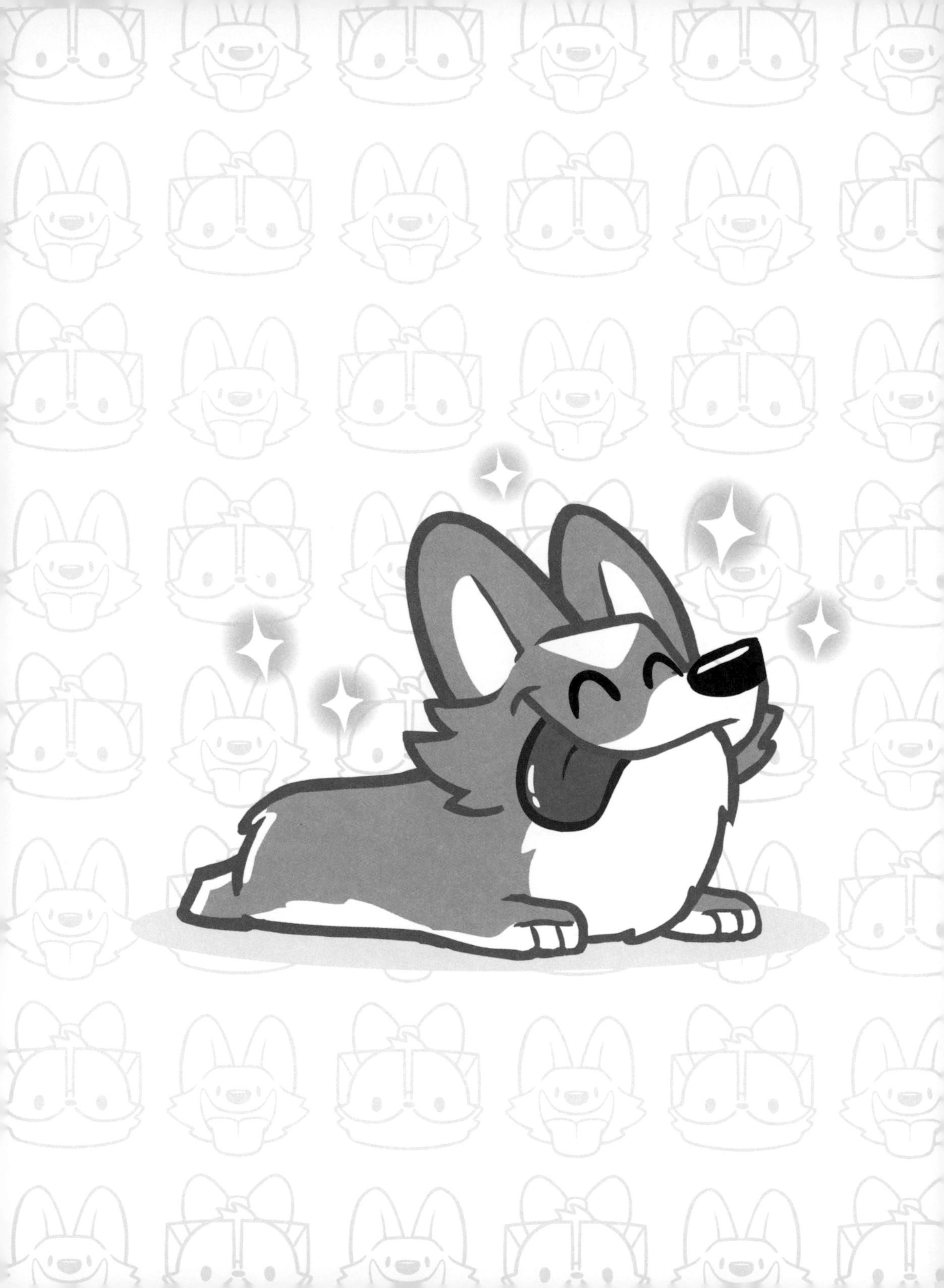

ABSOLUTELY CORGEOUS

LOVEABLE CORGI FEATURES

ADORABLY OVERSIZED
EARS

GIGANTIC SMILE

STUMPY
LITTLE LEGS

FLUFFY
ASSEMBLAGE
OF HAIR

PEANUT, YOU'LL NEVER MAKE FRIENDS WITH ALL THIS SHEDDING!

I TAKE THAT BACK.

CHUBBY LITTLE CORGI PAWS:

SO CUTE.

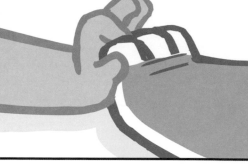

SO SOFT.

SO DELIGHTFUL.

PEANUT, YOU'LL FEEL BETTER
WHEN YOU'RE DONE.

SEE?

SOME SAY...

CORGIS ARE GOOD SWIMMERS,

BUT PEANUT DOESN'T TAKE ANY CHANCES.

ONE SLOTH'S TRASH...

IS ANOTHER DOG'S TREASURE.

DON'T BE JEALOUS, PEANUT.

YOU'VE GOT WIGGLE ROOM FOR CREATIVITY!

TERRIBLE GIFT IDEAS FOR A CORGI

SWING SET

LEG WARMERS

YOGA BALL

TROMBONE

IN A DOG-EAT-DOG WORLD

PEANUT DOESN'T MESS AROUND.

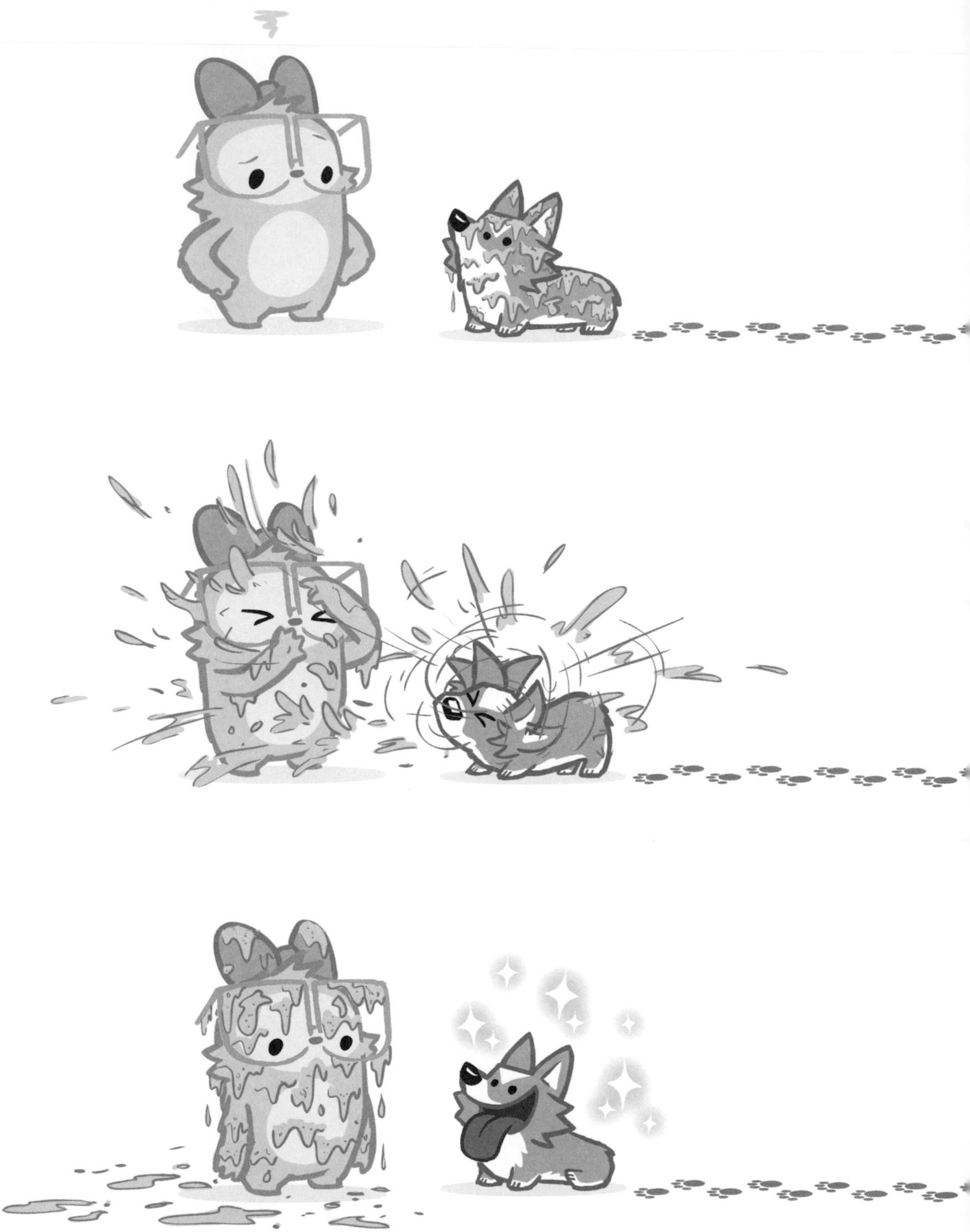

PEANUT LOVES BEING THE UNDERDOG,

ESPECIALLY AT NIGHT.

FUN FACT: A DOG'S SENSE OF SMELL IS 40X MORE POWERFUL THAN OURS.

WITH GREAT POWER, COMES GREAT RESPONSIBILITY.

PEOPLE THINK PEANUT'S BARK
IS BIGGER THAN HIS BITE.

I BEG TO DIFFER.

"THIS LOOKS LIKE A NICE PLACE TO SIT."

PEANUT'S A CONNOISSEUR OF U.F.O.'S

"UNIDENTIFIED FOOD OBJECTS"

SEE, CORGI LITERALLY MEANS
"DWARF DOG" IN WELSH.

TOLD YOU THIS WOULD WORK.

DOUBLE DUTCH, PEANUT!

OR KNOT.

MY SLEEPING BEAUTY

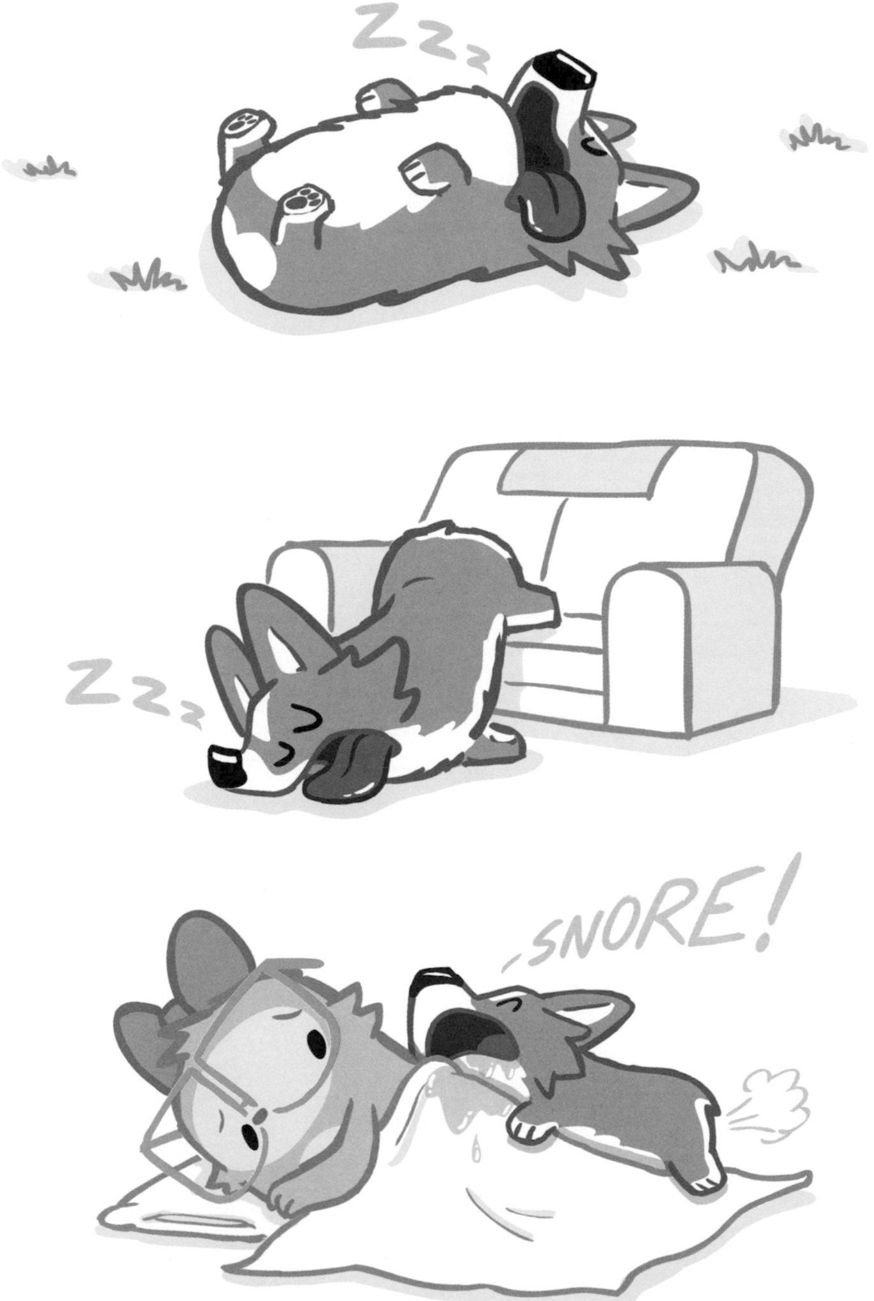
Z z z
Z z z
SNORE!

PEANUT'S SIGNATURE MOVE...

...IS HIS SIGNATURE.

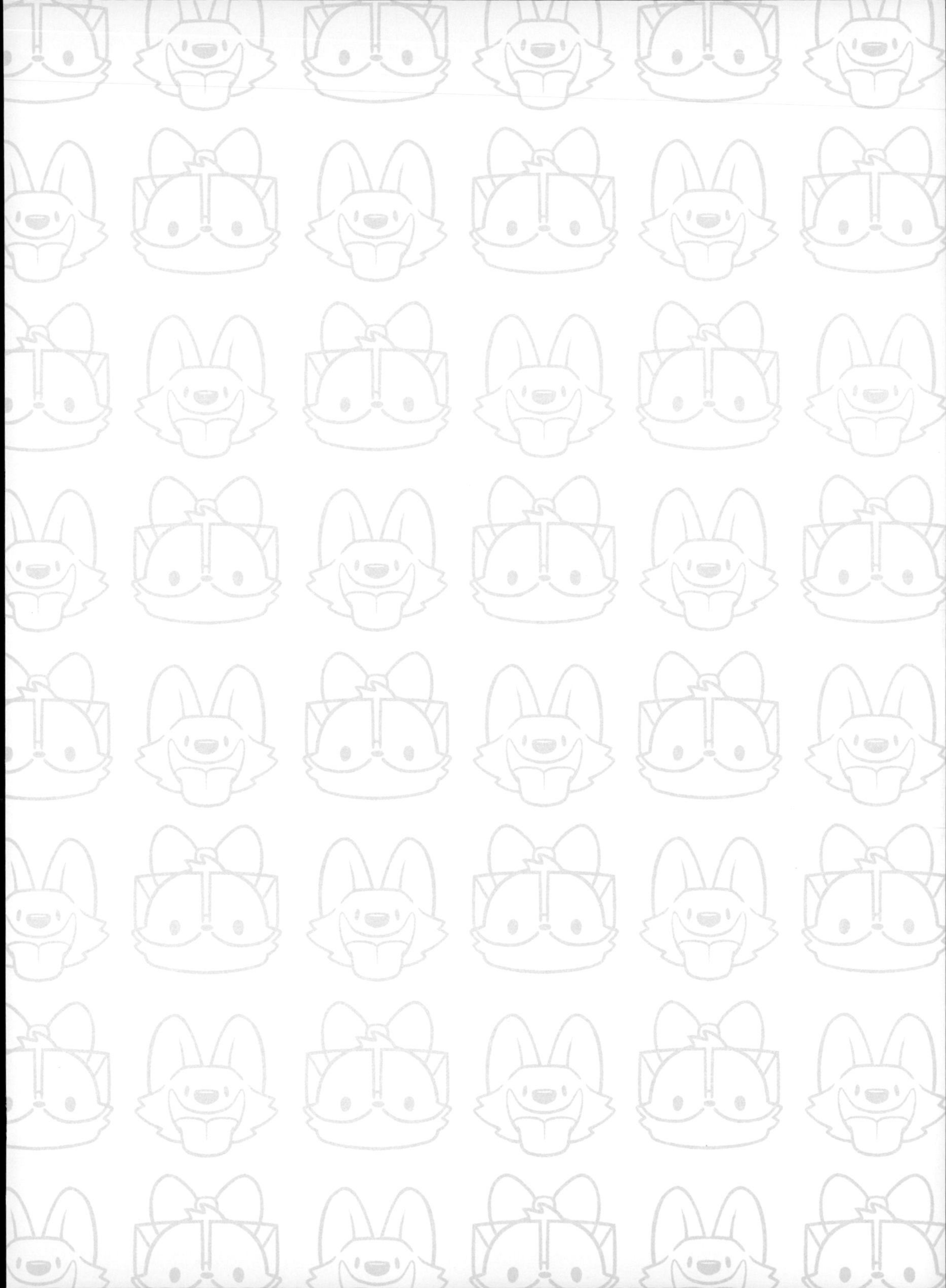

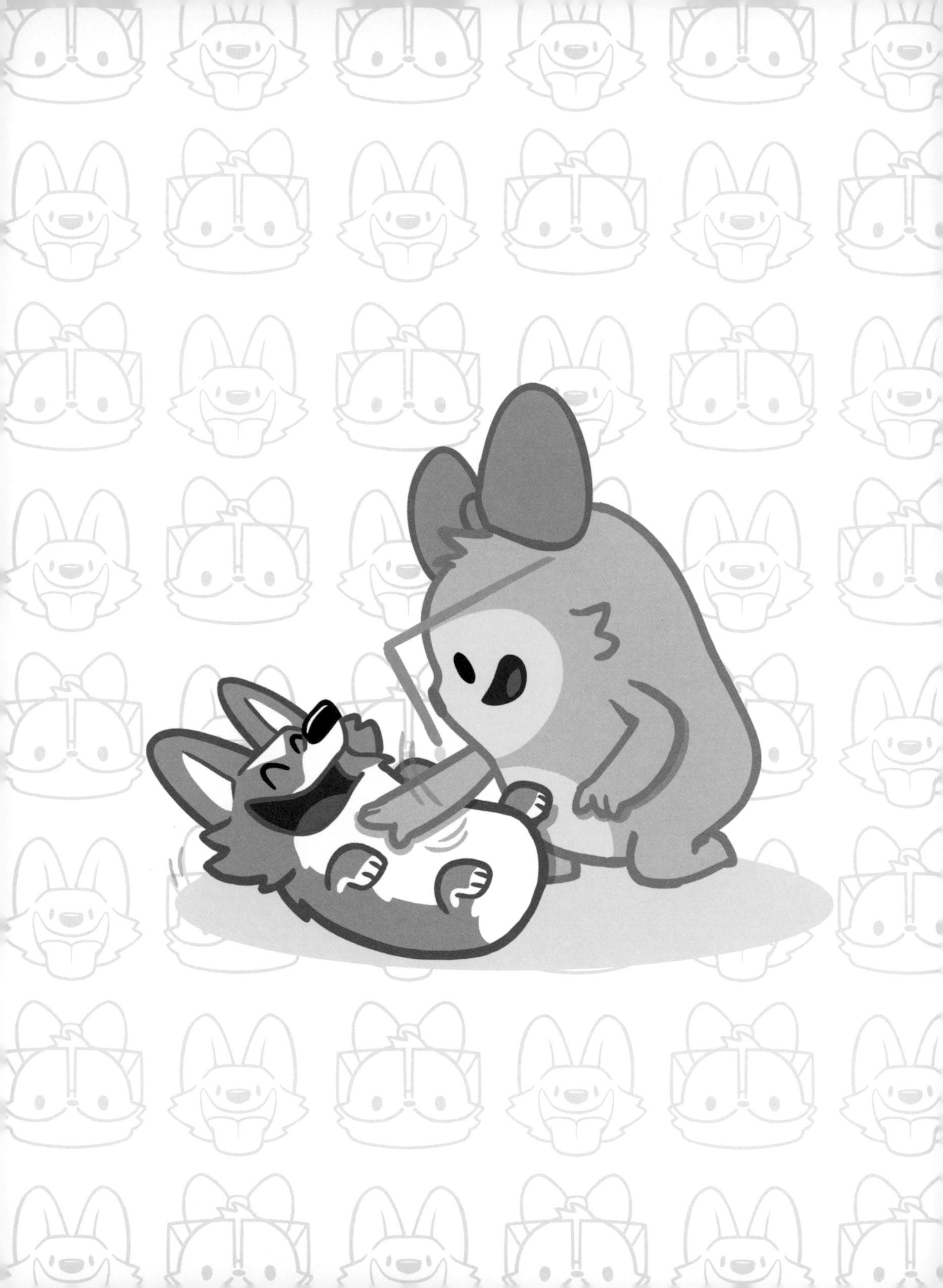

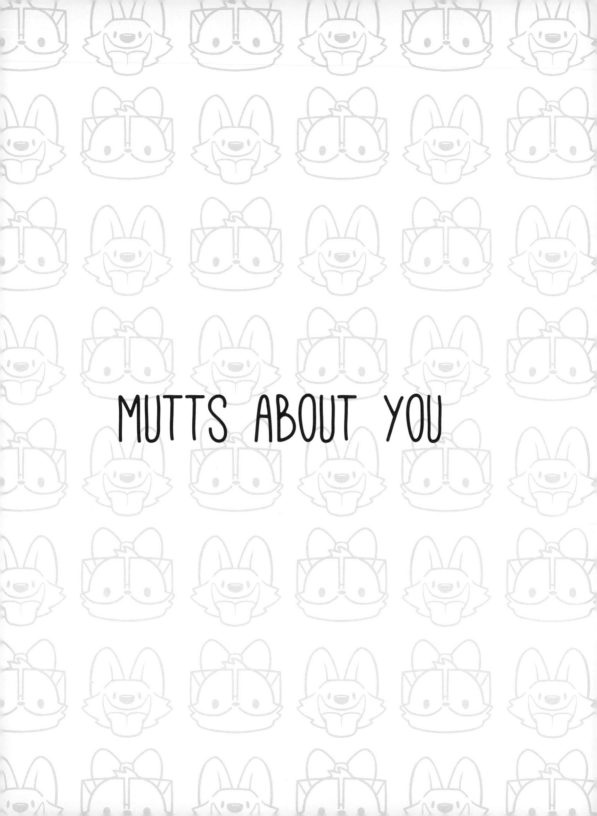

MUTTS ABOUT YOU

PEANUT:

SMALL BUT MIGHTY

SHORT BUT FAST

DERPY BUT THOUGHTFUL

Flower GARDEN

I APPRECIATE THE CONCERN, PEANUT,

BUT I THINK I'LL BE OKAY.

"ALONE TIME?"

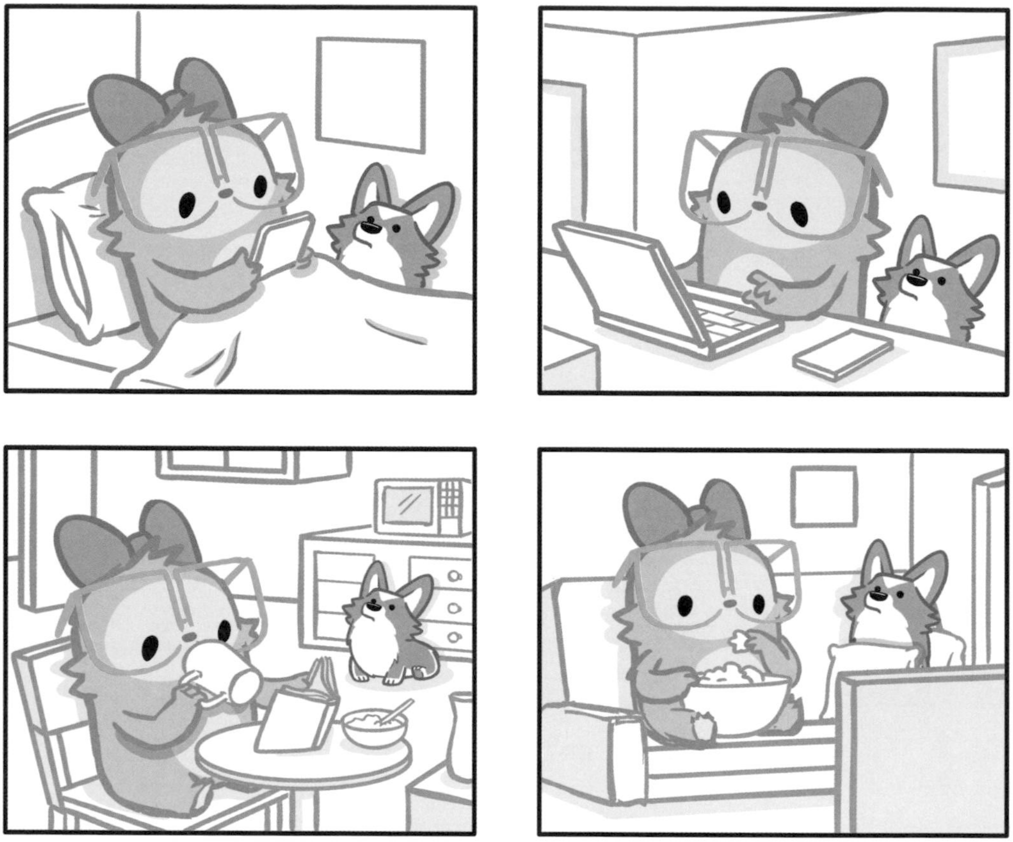

WHAT'S THAT?

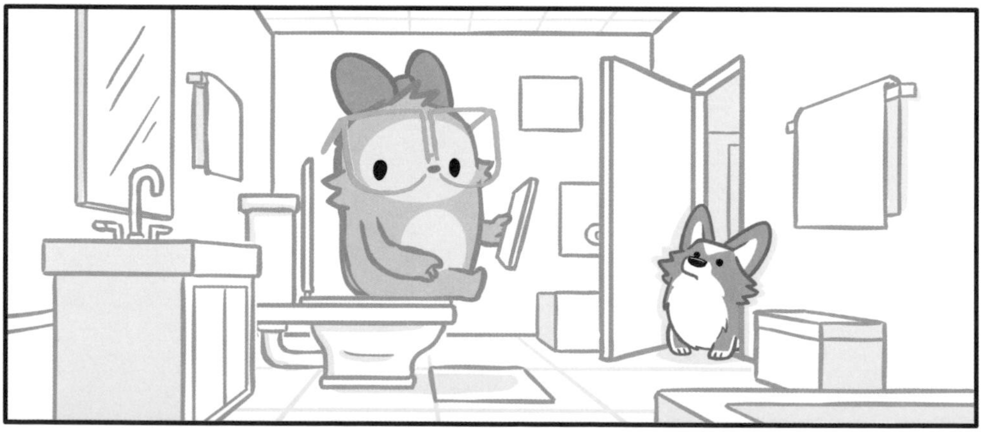

SORRY, PEANUT. I CAN'T PLAY RIGHT NOW.

FIND SOMEONE ELSE TO HANG OUT WITH.

WANNA GO FOR A WALK?

I'LL TAKE THAT AS A "YES."

PEANUT ONLY FOLLOWS ME FOR THE FOOD.

OR MAYBE HE LOVES ME FOR ME?

GUESS I'LL NEVER KNOW.

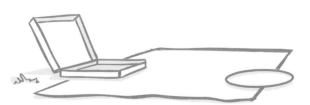

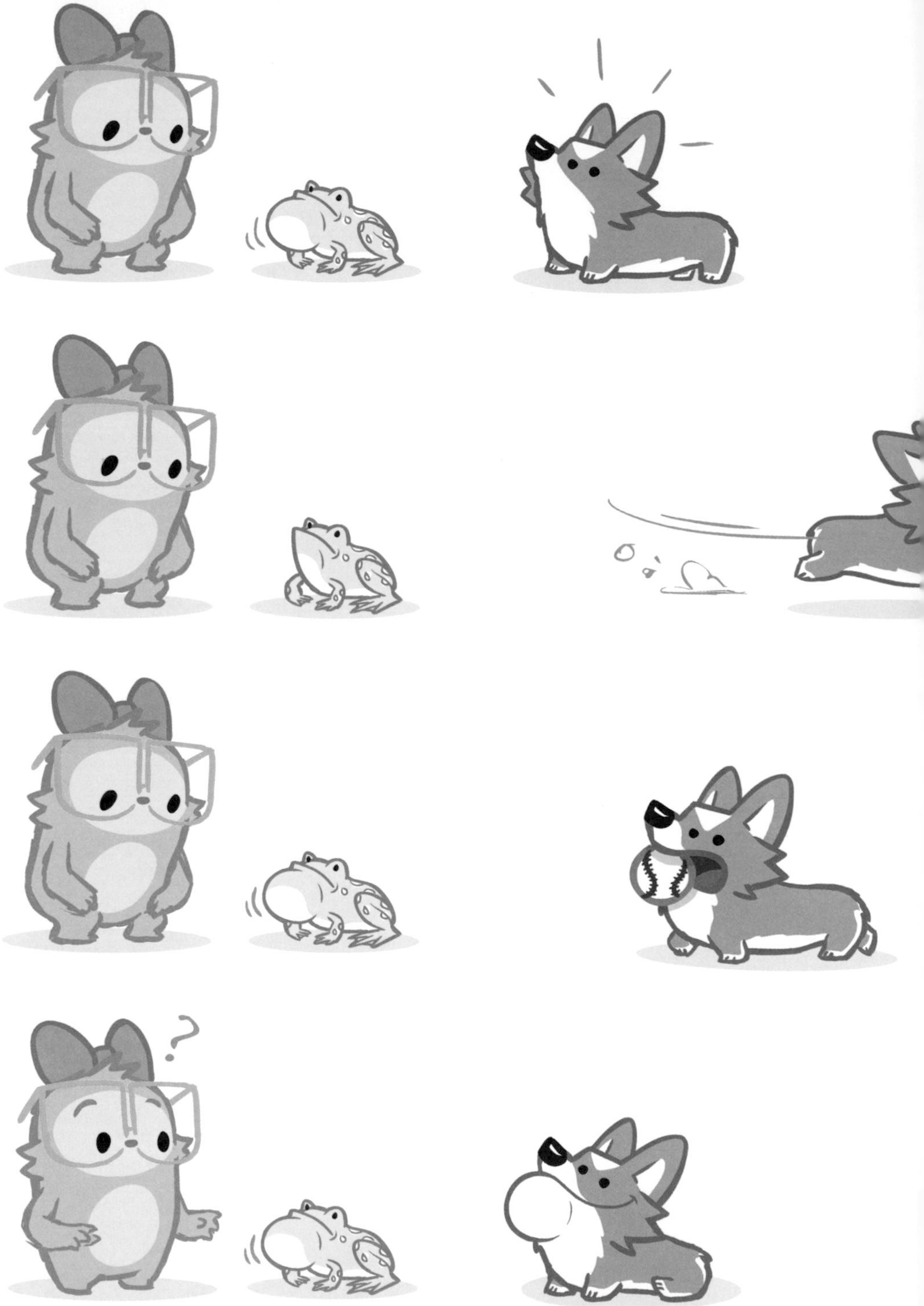

WHEN PEANUT GETS JEALOUS, HE...

1. BARKS

2. CROWDS MY SPACE

3. MISBEHAVES

4. LEAVES THE ROOM

5. COMES BACK TO WIN MY ATTENTION

PEANUT'S A MOUTH BREATHER.

HE REMINDS ME EVERY MORNING.

HOW I SEE LEFTOVERS:

HOW MY DOG SEES LEFTOVERS:

PEANUT'S A MASTER AT HIDE-AND-SEEK.

WELL...THE "SEEK" PART, AT LEAST.

THE 5-SECOND RULE IS A MYTH.

IT'S 2, ACCORDING TO PEANUT.

PEANUT'S BODY LANGUAGE EXPLAINED:

"SCRATCH PLEASE."

"FEED PLEASE."

"WALK PLEASE."

"STAY PLEASE."

NOTHING BEATS MY DOG'S LOVE AND AFFECTION,

EXCEPT FOR MAYBE A HOT SHOWER.

BE A GOOD WATCH DOG, PEANUT.

USE THESE TO KEEP AN EYE OUT.

THE SNIFF TEST

1. WHERE HAVE YOU BEEN?

2. WHO HAVE YOU BEEN WITH?

3. WHAT DID YOU DO?

4. WHATEVER.
   IS THIS FOR ME?

THINGS PEANUT LIKES LAUNCHING INTO:

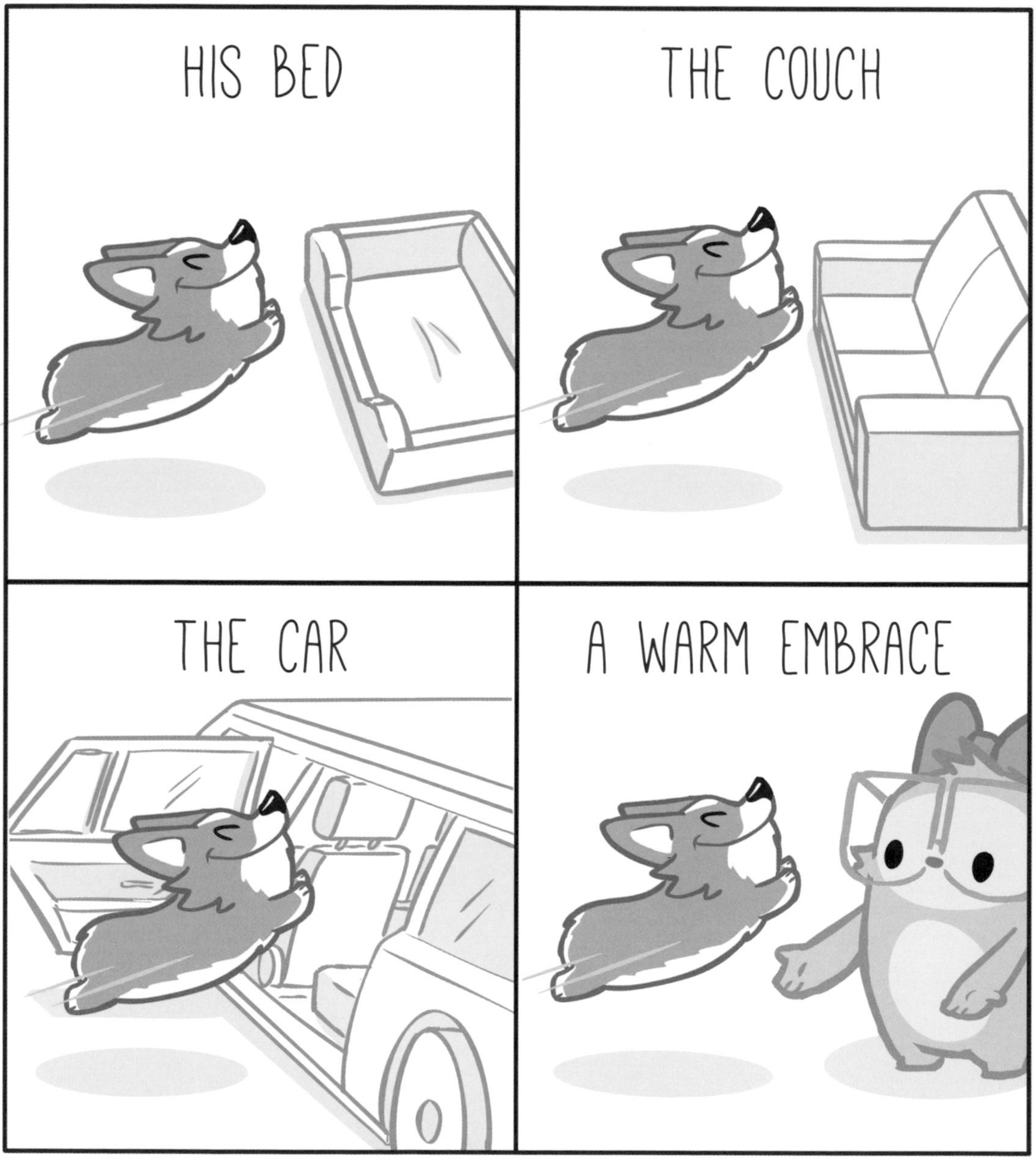
HIS BED
THE COUCH
THE CAR
A WARM EMBRACE

I LOVE YOU, MY LITTLE STINKY.

YOUR CUTENESS OVERPOWERS YOUR SMELL.

THE END

BUT WAIT...THERE'S MORE!

Did you know "Slothilda & Peanut" is an ongoing web-comic that's completely FREE online?

Get access to all the latest comics, cute stickers, behind-the-scenes content, and animations, when you subscribe to the newsletter!

Sign up at:

SLOTHILDA.COM

Also, be sure to follow "Slothilda & Peanut" on social media!
@slothilda

FUREVER GRATEFUL

This book was written/illustrated at the start (and in the middle of) two major life-altering events: the birth of my first child … and a global pandemic. Needless to say, it's been one heck of a ride filled with countless sleepless nights, bouts of tendonitis, and lots and lots of coffee.

This book wouldn't exist if it weren't for all the amazing people in my life who have provided a tremendous amount of support, encouragement, and love.

First, thank you to my agent, Mark Gottlieb, and the talented team at Trident Media Group for embracing my creativity and for helping me find the opportunities to keep this dream alive.

To my editor, Leah Zarra at Skyhorse Publishing. Thanks for believing in my vision and for giving me a second opportunity to showcase my work to the masses. You've been so patient, supportive, and kind throughout this journey.

To Benjamin Kaltenecker for helping me look over my first draft. Your brutal honesty and keen sense of humor helped me fine-tune this book. Thank you, brother!

Special shout-out to David Montejano, not only for being an amazing friend and avid supporter, but also for taking my author photo. Check him out on Instagram: @davemontejano. He's an incredibly talented photographer.

Big thanks to my creative collaborators Kate Pobuda, Lindsay Werner, Sara Kirshner, and Rebecca Evans for helping me bring Slothilda & Peanut to life in beautiful plush toy form.

Shout-outs to my family, friends, and supporters: Edwin Fabiero, Tita Annalin, Elisa and Peter Sio, Lindy Fabiero, Max Paronelli, Rhea Lampa, Karin Fabiero, Amro and Rowena Albanna, Fred and Lynn Villoria,

Joanne Kanemaki, the Enriquez family, Mikey and Lori Villoria, the de Claro family, Chris Robertson, Bradford Gibbons, Paul Yoshida, Nickolas Chelyapov, Lucas Gray, Elliot Grossman, Gio Cardenas, Brad and Russ Curry, Andy Huang, Liza Epps, Josh and Jo Kuanfung, Sam Choi, Amy Johnson, Marti Petty, Mary Lang, and Nadine Macaluso.

Most of all, thank you to my #1 advisor, who also happens to be the funniest and smartest person I know, my wife K.C. Thanks for cheering me on and supporting me every step of the way— all while being the most amazing mother to our little baby. You and Freddie are my world.

Thank you to Peanut, my other baby, and the real-life corgi whom the character in this book is based on. Peanut is my primary source of inspiration. He's also the cutest, most endearing fur ball around—always by my side, keeping me company throughout this entire journey. Without him, these comics wouldn't be nearly as fun to draw.

Lastly, an extra special thank you to my fans and readers. I am (and will always be) eternally grateful for your support. I wouldn't want to do this without you!

—Dante

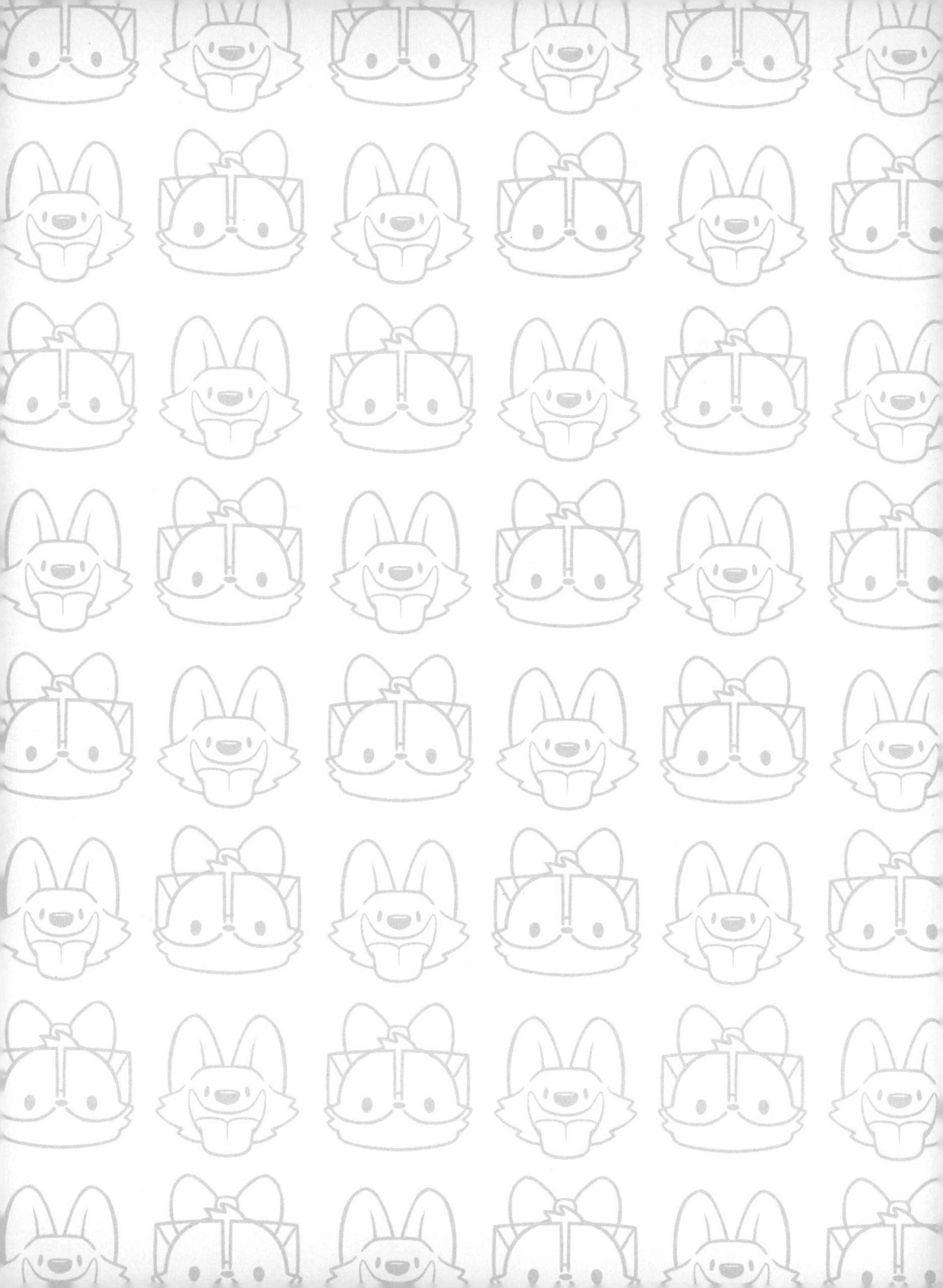

ABOUT THE AUTHOR

Photo Credit: David Montejano

Dante Fabiero is a Los Angeles-based author/animator and a graduate of the University of Southern California. Over the past ten years, Dante has worked in the animation industry on shows including *The Simpsons*, *The Cosmos*, *American Dad*, *Disenchantment*, and *Bless the Harts*.

In 2014 he started an online comic series about a sleepy little sloth named Slothilda, which quickly became a viral hit. Since then, his work has garnered more than 2 billion views on the popular GIF sharing platform, Giphy.

His first book, *Slothilda: Living the Sloth Life*, can be found wherever books are sold.

To get in touch with Dante, see more of his work, and subscribe to receive future comics for free, visit SLOTHILDA.com.

Skyhorse Publishing books may be purchased in bulk at special discounts for sales promotion, corporate gifts, fund-raising, or educational purposes. Special editions can also be created to specifications. For details, contact the Special Sales Department, Skyhorse Publishing, 307 West 36th Street, 11th Floor, New York, NY 10018 or info@skyhorsepublishing.com.

Skyhorse® and Skyhorse Publishing® are registered trademarks of Skyhorse Publishing, Inc.®, a Delaware corporation.

Visit our website at www.skyhorsepublishing.com.

10 9 8 7 6 5 4 3 2 1

Library of Congress Cataloging-in-Publication Data

Names: Fabiero, Dante, 1983- author.
Title: I love you more than my phone : a "Slothilda & Peanut" comic collection / Dante Fabiero.
Description: New York, NY : Skyhorse Publishing, [2020]
Identifiers: LCCN 2020036149 | ISBN 9781510759077 (hardcover) | ISBN 9781510759084 (ebook)
Subjects: LCSH: Friendship--Humor. | Sloths--Humor. | Pets--Humor. | American wit and humor, Pictorial.
Classification: LCC PN6231.F748 F33 2020 | DDC 818/.602--dc23
LC record available at https://lccn.loc.gov/2020036149

Cover design by Daniel Brount and Dante Fabiero
Cover illustration by Dante Fabiero

Print ISBN: 978-1-5107-5907-7
Ebook ISBN: 978-1-5107-5908-4

Printed in China

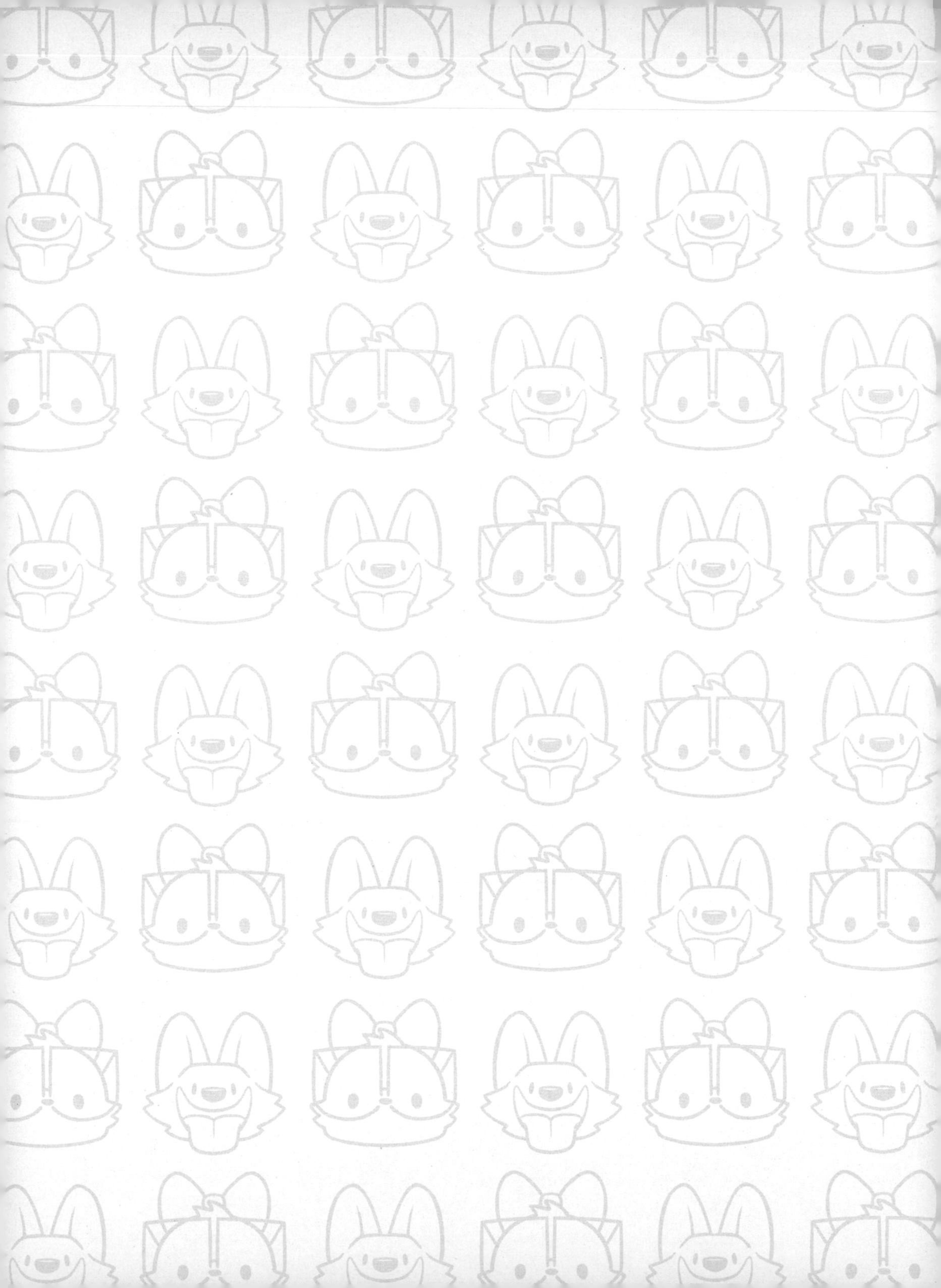

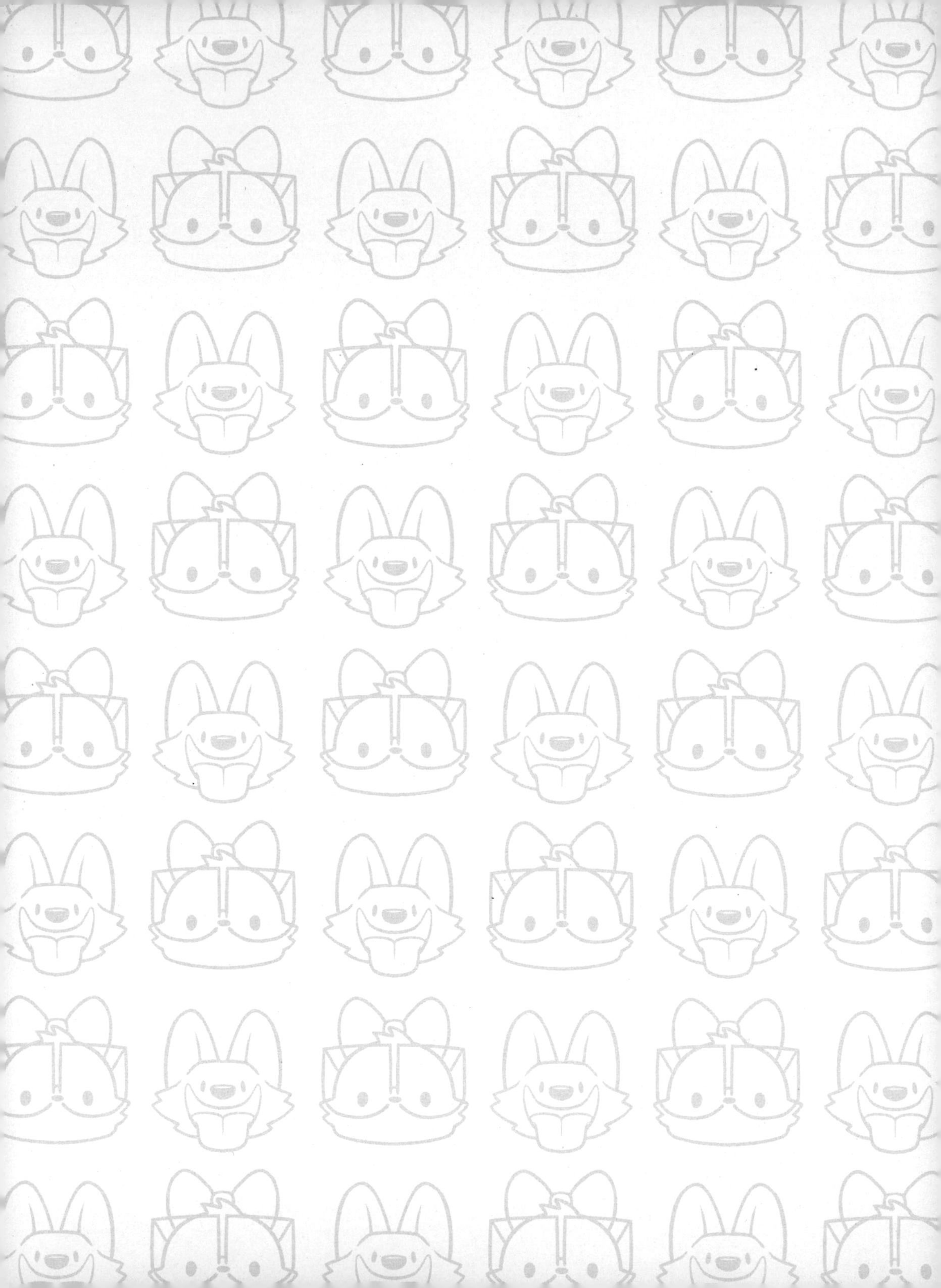